Investing

A Comprehensive Manual On Wealth Accumulation
Through The Creation Of A Diversified Investment
Portfolio Utilizing Exchange-traded Funds (ETF's) And
Selecting Individual Stocks

Ruben Matias

TABLE OF CONTENT

Introduction

It was only as I approached the age of thirty that I began to genuinely contemplate the ramifications of making investments for my future. Regrettably, it is frequently observed that Americans tend to delay their contemplation of financial investments for their future. Approximately 50% of the American population comprises individuals with no investments made, while an additional 33% have not accumulated sufficient savings to support their retirement expenses. I consider myself fortunate to have realized the significance of investing at a comparatively young age, and I now serve as evidence that individuals can make strategic investments that yield short-term benefits, as well as substantial long-term returns.

There exists a plethora of investment opportunities that have the potential to yield income in both the near and distant future. Through my personal findings, I have ascertained that the most suitable investments for my preferred way of living are those that generate prompt cash flow. Consequently, it is my utmost desire to impart this knowledge onto you. The objective of this book is to elucidate the merits of investment and provide guidance on strategic investment strategies capable of yielding diverse outcomes. Whether your ultimate objective is to fund your retirement, accumulate savings for a real estate investment, or enhance your financial safety net, I present tailored solutions to effectively assist you in achieving your goals.

If you do not start investing, then you will forever be reliant on your immediate income and the assistance of the state. Both of these sources of income lack long-term reliability, and the merits of saving should not be underestimated, even when one is young and fully employed. Whether one seeks financial security during unforeseen circumstances with a six month emergency fund, or aims to cultivate a yearly growing fund designated for leisure activities such as vacations, investing offers pragmatic benefits in terms of safety and entertainment, making it a valuable pursuit for individuals of all ages.

Throughout the subsequent chapters, you will acquire knowledge regarding the foundational principles of investment, along with the practical techniques and strategies for engaging in investment activities. Irrespective of the amount, be it one hundred dollars or ten thousand, various investment prospects exist that can be initiated at present, with enduring benefits extending well into the future. It is now opportune to deploy your dormant funds to foster the expansion of your savings and secure a more prosperous future for you and your loved ones.

Continue perusing and before long, you will witness the accelerated growth of your financial reserve.

Other Investment Possibilities

You possess certain resources that have the potential to generate income either through sales or by steadily appreciating in value over time.

Certain opportunities may seem unconventional, while others have the potential to be transformed into a consistent and enduring source of income.

This achievement may be attained due to their increasing value over time, their scarcity, or the possibility of encountering a buyer willing to offer a substantial sum for your assets.

They can be assets that can be sold for a profit, or assets that should be retained for an extended duration due to their potential for appreciating in value over time.

Let us now examine the most commonly recognized types.

Antiques And Collectibles

Antiques and collectibles offer a more favorable investment return due to their immunity to fluctuating inflation rates and stock market performance.

The value of collectibles remains constant, increasing only in proportion to the rarity and quality of the item.

They have the potential to deliver exceptional returns over an extended period. One should consider seeking the advice of experts or cultivating a broad understanding.

A selection of premium items and valuables suitable for investment purposes includes timepieces, currency, photographic equipment, graphic novels, postal artifacts, fine spirits, and board games.

According to the website sammydvintage.com, an article states that a Pinner Qing Dynasty container, valued at $80.2 million, holds significant global significance as a collectible item of immense importance.

The primary step in identifying and appraising antiques and collectibles is frequently

Determining the creator of the object by examining an impression or autograph.

Upon acknowledging classical furnishings, it is crucial to ascertain the authenticity and era of the piece.

The greater the inherent value of the initial object in its unaltered state, the lesser the modifications deemed necessary for maximizing its worth.

If you require an appraisal of collectibles, a reputable establishment to consider would be antiquated auctions, where experienced appraisers are present. Upon providing the item or sending photographs, they are generally willing to offer a complimentary valuation, under the expectation that you will subsequently consign your items with them for sale.

The differentiation between collectible and vintage items pertains to their respective ages. Antique items typically possess an age of approximately one century.

Advantages are:

• You are able to procure any items for the purpose of ventures.

• Rare items tend to gain value over an extended period • Unusual things have a tendency to appreciate in value over time

• They possess physical form or presence.

• They have the ability to be easily transported.

• Global investments

• Attain a level of capital appreciation that surpasses the standard rate of inflation

• You have the opportunity to participate in your investment.

• High-quality products

• Stylish

Disadvantages:

• The antique market lacks regulation

• Should you genuinely aspire to retrieve the funds that have been restricted due to your speculation,

There is no guarantee that they will be sold at the prices you desire.

• They can come with an astonishingly high price tag.

• Volatile industry

• Costly to maintain, keep up with, and store

You can locate and acquire collectibles through online platforms, retail establishments, and even auctions. You have the option of selling them on an online platform.

Cars

Are you able to retrieve cash from vehicles? When contemplating such investments, one likely considers the market for classic automobiles or vintage vehicles.

You can also explore opportunities to generate income from your vehicle through its rental for special occasions such as weddings.

Numerous individuals regard an automobile as a financial investment due to its substantial cost; however, investments generate monetary returns. Over time, a vehicle experiences depreciation and undergoes annual deterioration.

Despite the increasing reputation of vintage automobiles over the past three decades, investing in a classic engine is not a reliable means of attaining a respectable financial return.

If you are interested in investing in automobiles, it is imperative to carefully consider a vehicle that aligns with both your financial parameters and desired condition.

The majority of vehicles do not typically yield a profitable return, as their value depreciates immediately after being driven away from the dealership. However, in contrast, vintage automobiles experience an increase in value as time passes.

Vehicles that possess genuine historical or cultural value have the potential to become highly sought-after collectibles, especially when their rarity and aesthetic appeal are taken into consideration.

The automotive industry is indicative of the artistry market. It is an aesthetically pleasing speculation that you admire.

This constitutes significant personal property, and you will be liable for capital gains tax should you sell it for a profit.

You have the option of acquiring a brand new or gently used automobile, as you anticipate its potential to become a collectible in the foreseeable future. However, it is important to acknowledge the inherent risks involved in this endeavor.

Advantages of vehicle investment:

• Essence and demeanor

• Driving experience

• Personal enjoyment

Drawbacks of investing in a vehicle:

• Financial outlay

• Maintenance

• No mod-cons

• Depreciation

You have the option of searching for a superior-quality vehicle on the internet.

Credit Scores and Financial Intermediaries

The financial institution or authorized entity will assess your credit report to ascertain the projects for which you qualify. Your FICO score will enable the bank to assess your reliability in managing financial obligations. In the event that your score exceeds expectations, you will be eligible for the opportunity to acquire your home without the need for a down payment or with a loan-to-value (LTV) ratio of 100%. As your score increases, your initial investment decreases and you secure more favorable loan fees.

Several moneylenders do not provide zero down financing, while a substantial number of them do. This is a primary factor that motivated me to initially engage a financing intermediary in my professional career. They diligently explore numerous sources of credit and exert their efforts to secure a loan on your behalf. Typically, they charge a fee ranging from 0.5% to 1% of the total exchange amount and do not receive compensation unless you secure the loan. Do not allow the expense to excessively burden you, as professional services usually yield a higher return on investment compared to handling it independently, thereby offsetting their fees in the process. I currently rely predominantly on local lenders due to my established long-term lending relationships with them, which facilitate a more streamlined and expedited credit acquisition process.

Vendor credits and the mastery of the genuine zero-down transaction

Zero-down contract financing is readily available to numerous individuals due to the exceedingly competitive lending market, resulting in a growing number of homeowners obtaining loans without any upfront payment.

The most commonly employed method by mortgage agents to arrange zero-down financing involves dividing the loan amount into a primary and a secondary mortgage. Specifically, the primary mortgage accounts for 80% of the required loan amount, while the secondary mortgage makes up the remaining 20%.

Zero-down agreements are an exceptional tool to employ, even if you have accumulated funds for a down payment. By opting for the zero-down agreement, the funds initially allocated for the down payment can now be allocated towards the closing costs associated with the loan, expenses related to the relocation, purchasing new furniture, or any other financial obligations you may encounter upon transitioning into your new residence.

By virtue of an authentic contract that requires no initial payment, it won't be necessary for you to contribute any personal assets at the time of closing. To achieve this objective, one may opt for a cost-plus contract, albeit an expensive option, or alternatively, have the dealers bear the burden of closing costs.

It is imperative to comprehend that while it may serve as the primary means by which a borrower can purchase a home, a contract with zero down payment is associated with an elevated premium rate. In the end, your ultimate goal should be to initiate a renegotiation process once there is a significant increase in value, to achieve a loan-to-value (LTV) ratio of 80%.

Income-to-Debt Ratio

When purchasing an investment property, the primary challenges to overcome revolve around devising the initial capital and generating sufficient income to support the ensuing debt. The final alternative is commonly referred to as the ratio of payment to obligation.

Multiple financial institutions allow a maximum of 44% of your income to be allocated towards debt. This encompasses Mastercards, auto loans, residential mortgages, and investment property mortgages. It is not arduous to conceive the impact of an additional vehicle installment in raising your income-to-debt ratio and detrimentally influencing your eligibility for a bank loan.

You may be contemplating the viability of purchasing an investment property given your current income and expenses. There is no necessity for you to qualify in isolation. The investment property will generate income, which can be employed to offset the mortgage payment. In any event, financial institutions commonly only accept 75%

of the income, thereafter deducting the principal, interest, insurance, and utility expenses from that rental amount. The differentiating factor will lie in the overall remuneration (or adversity) that allows for adjustments to one's earnings.

That may appear somewhat exhilarating, nevertheless fundamentally it is rather straightforward. Consider if you were to purchase a four-unit loft priced at $200,000. The monthly remuneration and prevailing rental rates amount to $550 per unit, or a total of $2,200. In order to calculate your revised monthly income, you must augment your total rental revenue by .75, or 75 percent. The monthly remuneration provided by your financial institution has been amended to $1,650.

Presently, it is expected that you will be required to make an initial investment amounting to 10% of the total, in addition to entering into a contractual agreement that spans a duration of 30 years. Based on those circumstances, the monthly payment for your combined principal and interest will amount to approximately $1,200. In addition to the aforementioned, there is a monthly local charge of approximately $200 and a monthly protection fee of around $100. For bank

For the purpose of qualification, your cumulative expenditures amount to $1,500. Deduct the specified amount from your monthly income of $1,650, and subsequently incorporate this additional $150 into your salary earnings to enhance your eligibility for the loan. In the forthcoming Chapters 4 and 5, I will elucidate the methodology to determine your precise income and expenses. For the time being, it is imperative to gain awareness of the factors that the bank will evaluate as income.

Error: Placing unwavering trust in all written content.

Let us adopt a candid approach. The overwhelming majority exhibit a lack of intelligence. Additionally, should you choose to solicit advice from those individuals, you will undoubtedly find yourself immersed in a realm of immense suffering.

I believe we are currently facing a significant problem of information overload. The internet is remarkable as it provides copious amounts of information and greatly simplifies our lives. However, it is pertinent to note that this phenomenon can also present significant challenges and adversities in one's life. In what manner would you ascertain the veracity of the information encountered online or the accuracy of statements made by individuals? You don't. In the current era, it is essential that you acquire the skills to interpret and comprehend data independently.

Initiating the process of deciphering the relevant information necessitates initially heeding the advice of individuals successfully engaged in the same pursuits. One can reasonably assume that the majority of their statements are credible, considering their track record of achievements. However, if you find yourself participating in an online forum without any established mechanisms for verifying the credentials or credibility of the individuals involved or the information being shared, it is advisable to exercise caution. Even the most uninformed and inept individual can present themselves as an expert on the internet while disseminating false and misleading information.

Error: Taking into Consideration the Opinions of All Individuals in Your Surroundings "

Did I mention that there is a multitude of perspectives being voiced? Not only will excessively focusing on those around you likely result in a diminishment of your mental well-being, but it is highly probable that you will find yourself absorbing unfavorable guidance at some juncture.

I cannot ascertain whether or not you are aware, however it is common for people in our vicinity to have significant perceptions about the lives of others. I believe that it is, in fact, another customary experience for investors to encounter numerous individuals expressing their concerns and advising against engaging in real estate investment.

While I firmly believe in the prudence of attentively considering all advice received, for one cannot anticipate which counsel will truly pave the path to success, I also strongly advocate for assessing the credibility of the providers of such advice. Considering this, it is imperative for me to share with you the most potent notion that has guided me consistently in both my experiences within the realms of both the nation and commerce:

Do not seek guidance from individuals with whom you would not be willing to trade footwear.

One of the most notable examples of employing this assertion to aid me in determining from whom I should seek advice stems from my personal experience within my own family when I was endeavoring to engage in the realm of investing. My father consistently demonstrated a propensity for commencing tasks earlier than required, devoting himself diligently, economizing judiciously, and making secure contributions. He exerted considerable effort and displayed exceptional frugality. His sister, who happens to be my aunt, exhibited contrasting traits. She consistently served as a financial supporter, openly expended her funds, and engaged in ventures with risk. Both individuals' approaches led them to tremendous financial success. Upon developing a sense of curiosity in regards to investing, I discussed the matter with both individuals, and to my surprise, I received advice from both parties. The matter at hand pertained to the fact that each person's suggestion contradicted the advice of the others. To whom was I to be attentive?

Upon comparing the daily regimen I required, along with the experience, to the lives of both my father and my aunt, I found that my aunt's approach appeared to closely resemble my own preferences in a more pronounced manner. Although my father holds a significant place in my heart, I have yet to experience the need to diligently labor for someone else and meticulously save every penny I earn. Upon considering making a contribution, I prioritized the guidance provided by my aunt over that of my father. I heed my father's counsel in numerous aspects of life, albeit not when it comes to investing. Why? Since I have never required to interchange shoes with him in that domain. However, I am willing to trade shoes with my aunt who works in the contributing department. Given the circumstances, I opted to seek advice from the person with whom I intended to exchange shoes, as it appeared to be the most logical course of action.

An additional example of when this assertion played a fundamental role in my life was when it became pivotal in my journey towards becoming an entrepreneur. When I first became intrigued in real estate investment, which subsequently led to the establishment of my business, I encountered

An individual observed during a negotiation session who appeared to be leading a life that I perceived to be fantastical. He possessed an independent entity, providing him with the flexibility to determine his work schedule and travel as required. He demonstrated a lifestyle blueprint that closely mirrored my personal requirements. As a result, I consistently heeded every recommendation he ever offered me, and by doing so, I ultimately embarked on a business venture that afforded me all the same luxuries he enjoyed. I would consider swapping shoes with him, hence, I accorded him my attention. An alternative way to express the same sentiment in a formal tone could be: "The alternative approach would have involved seeking guidance on how to lead a life of personal autonomy, detached from the influence of an individual donning formal attire and occupying a desk during the standard business hours of Monday through Friday, from nine to five."

Does not seem to possess authenticity, does it?

What is the definition of a short-term rental?

A temporary rental refers to a fully furnished unit or property provided for a brief duration, typically encompassing rental periods that do not exceed 30 days. If the duration of the property rental is less than 30 days, it would fall under the classification of a short-term rental.

What is Airbnb?

Airbnb serves as a reputable platform for individuals and property owners to conveniently list their properties for short-term rentals, thereby generating income through such arrangements.

Whom does the term 'Airbnb host' refer to?

A host fulfills the dual role of serving as the personal assistant to the guest, in addition to being the individual who offers the rental space. Once you have listed a property on Airbnb, you are immediately regarded as the host. Moreover, this implies that you will be engaging in guest communication and offering hospitality services. Running an Airbnb enterprise entails being engaged in the realm of hospitality, necessitating a commitment to maintaining high-quality customer service and ensuring the constant satisfaction and well-being of your clientele.

What is rental arbitrage?

Rental arbitrage entails the practice of leasing properties and subsequently subleasing them through short-term rental platforms such as Airbnb and Homeaway. We will provide a more comprehensive discussion on this matter in subsequent paragraphs in accordance with the outlined course objectives. In essence, property searching, landlord communication, and mutually consenting to a sublease arrangement constitute the fundamental elements of this process. It presents a favorable opportunity for those who are reluctant to allocate substantial financial resources into this enterprise.

And finally, in order to generate passive income and attain financial prosperity and autonomy through this venture, it is imperative that you acquire the skills necessary to mechanize and streamline the operations of your Airbnb business. Therefore, it is advisable to diligently strategize and assemble your team prior to the commencement of your business venture.

Transitioning to the topic of the initial investment, it is imperative to possess a comprehensive understanding of your financial figures, particularly when embarking upon this venture. Engaging in reckless expenditure without proper deliberation will result in a lack of oversight and an inability to adhere to the designated budget. Allow me to explain that we are currently engaged in the practice of rental arbitrage. We have diligently searched for a suitable rental property and successfully engaged in negotiations with the landlord, securing a monthly rental fee of $1,500. The primary course of action to undertake in relation to the initial investment would involve remitting payment for the rental amount corresponding to the first month. To initiate the lease agreement, it is necessary for you to provide the landlord with an initial payment of $1500, in addition to a deposit which may vary depending on the specific property, typically around $800. Certain properties may necessitate a reduced deposit, whereas others may require a deposit ranging from $1,000 to $1,500.

Now, it is essential to include the costs associated with utilities. It is important to note that in this line of business, one must account for expenses related to utilities such as water, sewerage, electricity, internet connectivity, and other similar services. The estimated installation cost for this service would range from $100, as it requires soliciting various companies for their assistance. Additionally, it is likely that a deposit, potentially around $20 per utility, would be requested by the service providers. Therefore, you can simply provide an estimate of $100. Subsequently, we turn our attention to LLC, with the important caveat that participation in this particular entity is discretionary. It is not imperative to establish an LLC during the initial stages, but if you choose to do so, it is likely that you will incur costs ranging from approximately $30 to $1,000. It amounted to a total of $812 for our friend to establish his LLC, thus we plan on incorporating this expenditure into our overall costs.

City permits are contingent upon whether your municipality mandates upfront payment for permits or any other prerequisites necessary to engage in this business lawfully. In San Diego, any amount exceeding $600 will entitle you to acquire the necessary permits. Next, let us commence discussion regarding the furnishings. As a proprietor of an Airbnb enterprise, it will be incumbent upon you to bear the financial burden of procuring the furniture and covering all initial expenditures necessary for guaranteeing the occupancy and rental readiness of the property for Airbnb purposes. Regarding furniture, the expenses may vary based on the dimensions of your residence; however, we shall provide an approximate estimate of $3,000 to $3,500. Please find below an equation that can assist you in estimating an appropriate amount to allocate for furniture expenses: Rent multiplied by 2.5 equals the projected cost for furniture.

Consequently, the final amount tallies up to a total of $3,750. We will address the matter of the furniture cost at a later point, nevertheless, our approximate overall expenditure for the initial investment amounts to $7,562.

As evident from the presented information, commencing with a mere sum of $7,000 suffices, rendering a substantial initial investment unnecessary. If you have an interest in determining how you will be able to recoup that amount, you may utilize this calculation: Divide the total initial investment by the number of months you desire to achieve breakeven point.

Suppose you initiated this investment with an initial sum of $7,562 and aim to recuperate your investment within a one-year timeframe.

The quotient of dividing $7,562 by 12 months amounts to $567.66 per month.

Please note that during the initial year or first few months, make every effort to recuperate.

It is essential to carefully consider your investment decisions, as indiscriminate expenditure without measuring the return on your initial capital investment or potential profitability may hinder your progress and impede future recovery efforts. The more expediently you recoup your investment, the sooner you will have the capacity to embark on another Airbnb venture.

The Prospects of Non-Fungible Tokens (NFTs) and Cryptocurrencies in the Coming Years

Numerous individuals held the perception that Bitcoin was a deceptive or transient phenomenon during its initial emergence. When Bitcoin gained widespread recognition among the general public, imprudent investors suffered substantial financial losses, while criminals exploited vulnerabilities in the infrastructure, thereby undermining the legitimacy of this digital currency. The initial coin offering (ICO) phenomenon resulted in a division, as Bitcoin (BTC) maximalists regarded the developments on Ethereum (ETH) with apprehension.

Following a period of reduced performance and an extensive acquisition of knowledge, accompanied by the widespread integration of efficient blockchain technologies, the prospects for bitcoin's future now appear exceptionally promising.

Blockchain revolutionizes our interactions and perceptions of money, finance, and currency, exerting its influence on policymakers and individuals in positions of authority. Its existence is no longer contingent upon the downfall of traditional banking markets. Cryptocurrencies exhibit greater performance compared to conventional banking systems, owing to a wide array of user-friendly fiat currency gateways and decentralized applications on-ramps.

Over an extended period, the traditional economic markets have endeavored to cultivate a negative perspective on cryptocurrencies; however, hedge funds, banks, governments, and businesses are now progressively embracing the potential of Blockchain technology.

The adoption of cryptocurrencies will become commonplace and pervasive as traditional financial institutions and banking establishments continue to employ blockchain technology. Cryptocurrencies have the potential to emulate the success of established payment systems like PayPal and Apple Pay, and eventually attain a position of widespread adoption as the industry norm.

They are revolutionizing the gaming industry, making it possible to embark on global tours using their platform. In due course, blockchain technology is likely to find application in insurance, mortgages, and various other sectors. Cryptocurrencies no longer pose a threat to the traditional financial system; instead, they are making progress and showing outdated institutions how to adapt to an era of technological and digital advancement. Simultaneously, they are presenting consumers with a pathway to achieve financial autonomy.

Publishing Your Property on Airbnb

Given that you are now in possession of furniture and property, it is advisable to proceed with the arrangement of listing your property on Airbnb. It can be easily accomplished. It is imperative that you obtain the necessary information and respond to the inquiries. Prior to proceeding, we kindly suggest visiting the website airbnb.com.

When enlisting your property on Airbnb, it is essential to compile essential details regarding the property, include high-quality photographs, accurately specify the number of bedrooms and bathrooms, and highlight the amenities and features available.

What constitutes a superior listing on the Airbnb platform?

Ensure that you possess a comprehensive and enticing description, a well-crafted title, high-quality imagery, a strategically advantageous location for your Airbnb, an ample assortment of amenities, and an appropriate pricing strategy. Do not set the price of your Airbnb too high, as this may result in a lack of bookings. Please ensure that you perform exceptionally well on this task, as doing so will undoubtedly maintain your consistent workload.

Strategies for Determining the Optimal Pricing for Your Airbnb Listing

Kindly direct your attention to this matter as it may become somewhat intricate. Initially, it is imperative for you to ascertain the precise extent at which your costs are equaled by your revenue, otherwise known as your break-even point. In order to acquire that information, supposing your rental costs alongside other expenditures amount to $2000, it can be divided by a period of 30 days. It is not necessary to include 31 in the calculation, since certain months comprise only of 30 days, which corresponds with your nightly rate. In order to achieve a breakeven point, a pricing of $66.66 must be established. That amount will be your daily tariff required to reach a point of equilibrium. If you consistently rent your Airbnb at this price on a daily basis, you will achieve a point of financial equilibrium.

It is advisable to generate a monthly profit of $1000 by utilizing the profit formula, encompassing both rental income and expenses. Now, integrate the desired profit margin of $1000, contingent upon the geographical location. Suppose we consider the average monthly earnings of a typical Airbnb to be around $3000. Additionally, you must include that as well.

Assuming the aggregate of rampless costs and the desired profit of $3000, is combined and subsequently divided by a duration of 30 days. This amounts to a daily rate of $100, providing you with your nightly accommodation cost.

To achieve a monthly income of a substantial amount, it is advisable to set a nightly fee of $100, ensuring a profitable outcome. It is possible to generate varying levels of income by setting a price of $100 on weekdays and increasing it to $140 on weekends. Subsequently, those additional $40 will accumulate. It provides a fundamental understanding of how to determine the appropriate pricing for your Airbnb rental.

When initiating your listings on Airbnb, it is advisable to ensure that your pricing is set at an appropriate level, as deviating from this could prove to be a costly error. Ensure that you secure the rental at a competitive price or achieve a marginal profit in order to attain a higher position in the search rankings. Subsequently, in due course, you may elevate your pricing. Now you are fully prepared to serve as a host on the

Airbnb platform. You acquired the property, furnished it, and subsequently listed it on the Airbnb platform. It is now necessary to access your calendar and establish appropriate pricing.

It is indeed exhilarating to have all preparations in order. It is advisable to include a cleaning fee for each stay. I recall when I first listed my property on Airbnb, I regrettably overlooked the inclusion of a cleaning fee. Consequently, numerous bookings were made without this essential charge. In essence, I encountered an unfavorable situation, but it is of no significant concern. Please ensure that you include a cleaning fee.

As previously stated, the rates are lower on weekdays compared to the comparatively higher prices on weekends. Furthermore, make preparations for the arrival of your inaugural visitor. There is no obligation for you to meet them. I am aware that a significant number of you will inquire about this matter. Is it necessary for you to personally greet your guest upon their initial arrival, for example, by providing them with a key? You are not obligated to do so, but you may choose to handle this remotely and ensure that you maintain a guest book.

Ensure that you are adequately prepared and equipped by providing a guest book containing essential information such as the wi-fi password, house regulations, as well as addressing any potential inquiries visitors may have, such as operating household appliances. Strive to attain the esteemed classification of super host.

By attaining super host status on the Airbnb platform, you can enhance your visibility and substantially increase your likelihood of being prioritized by potential guests in comparison to non-super hosts. Furthermore, it is imperative to prioritize the provision of exceptional customer service in order to achieve the esteemed status of a super host, and promptly address any inquiries posed by each individual guest.

Always Honor Reservations

This is another crucial aspect to consider, as the cancellation of reservations has the potential to result in the cessation of your Airbnb listing or hinder your progression towards achieving super host status on the platform. In addition, kindly reach out to each guest upon check-out and graciously request their consideration in providing a five-star review. This is the approach I used, which resulted in me achieving super host status in a remarkably short period.

Establishing an Effective Team and Implementing Business Automation

In order to achieve scalability and autonomize your business operations, it is imperative to assemble a capable and cohesive team. The individuals who hold the greatest sway in your team are the custodial staff, maintenance personnel, and a collaborating co-host. Engaging the services of a third-party company is not necessary for the role of a co-host. You may inform your acquaintance or an individual known to you residing in that particular city. Request their cooperation as a co-host, ensuring that they can act as a vigilant presence to monitor the property during any untoward incidents, with a mutually agreed remuneration arrangement. That is the entirety of their duty. Please ensure that you engage the services of one or possibly even two cleaners, maintenance staff members, and an additional co-host.

Implement automation for your Airbnb, devise a systematic turnover strategy, and arrange for professional cleaners to undertake post-checkout cleaning.

Foster a positive rapport with your cleaning staff, provide them with thorough training on your desired cleaning methods, and ensure smooth operations by ensuring they possess the necessary skills to effectively maintain the property.

Engage the services of a skilled tradesperson or an individual proficient in performing maintenance tasks. In the event of a bathroom blockage, one may contact the service providers, and subsequently settle the payment using digital platforms such as Venmo or Zelle upon completion of their tasks. It\\\'s that easy.

Lastly, it is advisable to consider having a co-host as they can undertake the responsibility of replenishing your inventory. They intend to purchase hygienic towels, bathroom tissue, as well as cleaning materials for your Airbnb. They have the ability to replenish inventory and address any personal matters on-site. Suppose a visitor experiences a challenging or difficult stay. A co-host possesses the ability to engage in conversation with them in order to assuage their emotions.

Furthermore, it is advantageous to implement an automated system for check-in and checkout procedures. There is no necessity for you to repeatedly travel to that location in order to deliver and retrieve the guest key. In order to furnish them with a code or alternatively utilize a lockbox, it is necessary to acquire a sophisticated smart lock. Guests may also avail themselves of a secured lockbox equipped with a uniquely assigned code, providing them independent access to the key. Thus, it is possible to automate all tasks.

Furthermore, it is imperative that you make every effort to prevent any unwelcome disturbances caused by visitors or gatherings. In light of this, it is advised to install noise-sensing cameras outside the premises and to engage in prior communication with these devices prior to each visitation. Kindly inform them that in the event they contravene the stipulated rule, a fee will be levied upon them. Inform them that noise detectors are in place to supervise and regulate the level of sound emanating from the premises. All of these factors will play a crucial role in the successful operation and automation of your Airbnb establishment.

Types Of Investor

What type of investor do you identify as?

• Pre-financial backer. An individual who has yet to make a contribution.

• Silent investor. • Indirect financial supporter. • Passive financier. • Non-participatory funder. • Inactive sponsor. An individual who actively contributes but relies on the expertise of others to enhance their financial growth. It is the option that offers a higher level of security. There are no negative aspects associated with being an inactive financial supporter. In essence, you are seeking to secure financial success.

• Engaged funding contributor. • Actively involved investor. • Participating financial supporter. •

Proactive patron. • Involved monetary sponsor. An individual who employs innovative approaches to understand and handle their conjectures, while independently creating opportunities tailored to their own objectives.

Main Types Of Investment

These categories represent the principal forms of investments:

• Shares

• Bonds

• Mutual Funds

• Index Funds

• Investment Funds

• ETFs, commonly referred to as Exchange-Traded Funds, • Exchange-Traded Funds, known as ETFs, • ETFs, an abbreviation for Exchange-Traded

Funds, • Exchange-Traded Funds, a term often used to describe ETFs, • ETFs, which are also known as Exchange-Traded Funds

• Fixed-term deposit accounts (FTD)

• Property

• Cash

• Options

• Futures

• Annuities

• Retirement

• Assets

• Cryptocurrencies

• Commodities

• Currencies

Hedge Funds

A versatile investment refers to a collective investment fund that trades somewhat liquid assets and employs advanced trading strategies in order to enhance performance.

A mutual fund typically remunerates its portfolio manager through the payment of an administration fee and a performance fee.

Investors engaging in speculative stock investments must meet the criteria of being financially affluent backers who possess adequate qualifications.

It is believed that they possess awareness concerning the speculative opportunities and recognize them as a result of the potential gains.

The chief aims of speculative investments in stocks are to enhance returns and mitigate risk. Their intention is to generate profits irrespective of the market's upward or downward fluctuations.

They are frequently readily accessible for the purpose of authorizing financial investors. In order to be recognized as an accredited financial supporter, it is necessary to satisfy one of the subsequent criteria:

• Ensure an individual payment of $200,000 or higher solely for your own benefit

• It is required that you possess a personal net worth exceeding $1 million.

• The individual must hold a senior executive position, such as a chief executive officer or chief financial officer, actively involved in managing complex investments, or possess a representative interest plan or trust fund with a minimum value of $5 million.

The majority of speculative stock investments operate under a compensation structure known as the 2 and 20 model, wherein the mutual fund manager receives a 2% management fee based on the assets under management, along with a performance fee of 20%.

Types:

• Macro. Allocate capital into equities, fixed income securities, futures contracts, derivatives, and occasionally foreign exchange.

• Equity. Efforts to counteract declines in volatile markets by investing in equities or equity indices and subsequently divesting them.

• Investments with a multifaceted nature, involving the exchange of relative worth. Acquire assets that are anticipated to appreciate, while simultaneously divesting those likely to depreciate.

• Financially troubled mutual funds. They are frequently linked to credit disbursements or reorganization.

Hedge funds invest in real estate, commodities, currencies, derivatives, and various other assets. Therefore, they have the ability to allocate resources to any initiative they choose.

Benefits of a support fund: "Benefits derived from the establishment of a support fund:

• Flexibility. Mutual funds are not openly traded among individuals, thereby fostering greater flexibility, as they are not subject to oversight by a specific governing authority.

• Aggressive speculation technique. This is vital in order to achieve an elevated level of return.

• Enhances the opportunity for improvement. The asset has the potential to contribute to diversification and, in addition, reduce risk.

• Proficient counsel and transparency. The versatile investment administrators also possess expertise in matters of financial management.

The drawbacks of engaging in speculative stock investments include:

• Hedge store expenses. They enforce a fee model referred to as 2 percent and

20 percent. Investors are subject to a 2% administrative fee for the management of the fund. Moreover, they also remit a performance fee of 20% to the asset manager for any profits earned throughout the year.

• Potential hazards and rewards. They are perceived as engaging in a significant amount of risk-taking.

• Stocks or bonds tend to be more liquid in nature compared to them in general.

• It may only authorize the withdrawal of funds from your account after a predetermined period of time or at designated intervals throughout the year.

The initial investment amounts for mutual funds typically vary from $100,000 to in excess of $2 million.

It can be exceedingly challenging for individual investors to gain access to high-quality mutual funds; nonetheless, one may explore an alternative approach to invest in such funds. One could invest resources in the provision of a financial institution specializing in hedge funds.

CHAPTER 8: MONERO

K

Monero has gained recognition as a cryptocurrency distinguished by its unparalleled level of anonymity. This distinction arises from its steadfast commitment to upholding privacy, hence its reputation as a "privacy-coin."

In contrast to other cryptographic currencies, which rely on making transactions within the blockchain publicly visible, Monero prioritizes confidentiality by maintaining balance on the side of privacy.

The intricate cryptographic mechanisms employed by this currency to obfuscate sensitive information, such as user funds, identities, and addresses, render it an untraceable digital asset. Consequently, these cryptographic advancements have wielded a strong allure for cyber adversaries, over time, as they significantly facilitate the ability of these individuals to operate covertly and conduct illicit activities with a high degree of impunity.

Initially introduced as BitMonero, this digital currency was established in April 2014. While Monero was not at first influenced by the use of the CryptoNote protocol, which currently serves as the foundation for numerous other virtual currencies, it ultimately adopted this protocol. The utility of CryptoNote extends beyond its ability to guarantee a high level of transaction privacy, transaction amount confidentiality, and user anonymity. It also renders ASICs, specialized mining hardware, obsolete. The protocol's consistent updates impose significant costs on creating an ASIC capable of undermining Monero. As a result, numerous forks of the cryptocurrency have emerged over time, enabling this action. By means of clarification, an Application Specific Integrated Circuit (ASIC) is a type of integrated circuit that is capable of efficiently performing computational tasks within a significantly reduced timeframe, owing to the manipulation of electrical consumption well beyond the norm.

derivative of Bytecoin, an alternative option

Proven to be lucrative in the industry

The inherent nature of the blockchain as a distributed ledger does not provide adequate assurance of substantial levels of security, which is...

techniques employed by Monero inherently

The rationale behind the anonymization

Isolate it from other digital currencies. An instructive analogy to consider in terms of its temperament is akin to the ruler of cryptocurrencies, Bitcoin. This digital currency provides a form of pseudo-anonymity, wherein users' identities are not disclosed in the blockchain, but the transactions and associated amounts are transparent and accessible through a conventional block explorer. However, the notion of discernibility should not remain confined solely to interactions, as it is indeed feasible to trace the identities of the individuals in question through thorough examination. the intention behind this detectability is that when using BTC and other cryptocurrencies, users do not automatically generate new IP addresses for every transaction, whereas

CryptoNote necessitates the use of a location only once, and this location varies with every operation.

Irrespective of the chosen wallet, the reception of moneroj (plural of monero) occurs through the act of sharing the wallet's location, encompassing an alphanumeric code for duplication or a QR code for scanning, with the individual from whom the payment is to be collected. The amount is sent after entering or scanning the code and inputting the desired transfer amount. It is a remarkably uncomplicated approach that appears to adhere closely to the trading strategies employed by other cryptocurrencies.

Indeed, beneath these insignificant progressions lies a sophisticated anonymization component intricately linked to the implementation of the CryptoNote protocol.

In the present scenario, it is evident that there exist not only public and private keys, as the discussion entails various types of keys, including a set of keys for review purposes and another set of keys for shopping activities.

However, prior to proceeding with the depiction of this system, it is appropriate to introduce the concepts of double spending and strategic representation.

The risk of double spending does not solely pertain to Monero and involves the possibility of the same amount being spent twice, whereby identical resources are utilized for two separate transactions.

Insightful and Lucrative Educational Experiences

(1) It is advisable to conduct one's own assessment assurance, even in cases where an evaluation has not yet been completed, as appraisals may not always accurately predict the final selling price of a property.

(2) Ensure constant supervision over the watch manufactured by an employed artisan; in the event it is left unattended, there is a risk of potential compromise. If you are uncertain about whether something will comply with the applicable codes, it is advisable to seek the assistance of an individual who possesses expertise in adhering to the

regulations, for the purpose of inspecting the work.

(3) However, the example they incorporated authentically surpassed those two distinctions. They devised a method to exercise caution when dealing with the disrobed gentleman who generously donates his own garment. They should have been highly skeptical of an individual who displayed great expertise in identifying and facilitating alleged exceptional solutions, only to allow themselves to profit extensively from them. If those arrangements were truly exceptional to begin with, it raises the question as to why someone as knowledgeable and experienced as Rick did not personally execute those transactions. In this instance, it was determined that the deals were favorable solely due to Rick's successful identification of individuals who possessed financial resources and the

capacity to acquire mortgages. These transactions did not possess inherently advantageous attributes. A fool and his money will soon be parted. If the arrangements were truly exceptional, Jill and Linda would have been unaware of them as Rick, being a skilled individual, would have handled those preparations personally.

(4) Regrettably, the current situation is widely prevalent. A straightforward guideline to bear in mind, which can assist you in remaining vigilant against deceptive transactions disguised as "beneficial deals," is to exercise caution when presented with a real estate opportunity where someone else is readily offering it to you, requiring only your financial investment or credit. If the arrangement truly possessed such excellence, rest assured that it would have remained beyond your knowledge. Rare opportunities rarely present

themselves conveniently and effortlessly. The most optimal arrangements in real estate typically arise from the diligent efforts or superior acumen applied while independently uncovering and discovering them.

The New Normal And Business Growth Cycle

In the earlier discussion, we touched upon the cycle of business growth and the significance of identifying enterprises characterized by rapid rates of product adoption. Let us examine the historical progression of various technologies and their respective rates of adoption:

The telephone was created in the year 1876, however, it took nearly a century for landline telephones to achieve widespread adoption in households. In order for this to occur, extensive infrastructure development was necessary, coupled with the simultaneous expansion of the network effect to render the product meaningful and valuable to consumers.

Additionally, the telephone encountered the challenge known as the "last-mile problem," wherein the logistical complexities and costs escalated as the network extended its reach to end-users. Consequently, it was only during the 1960s that landline telephones were present in 80% of households in the United States.

The rapid uptake of microwave ovens, mobile phones, smartphones, various social media platforms, tablets, and other technological advancements in contemporary times is indicative of their widespread acceptance. The tablet computer exhibits the most prominent increase on the chart, experiencing a significant surge in adoption from almost nonexistent levels to approximately 50% within a span of roughly five years.

What are the reasons behind the rapid adoption of emerging technologies? It appears that this is partially attributed to the fact that contemporary technology relies on lesser infrastructure as opposed to the installation requirements of water pipes, cable lines, electricity grids, and telephone wires that were prevalent in the 20th century.

Moreover, this also signifies an additional characteristic of contemporary consumers - they possess a strong sense of connectivity, are prompt to take action, and exhibit a fearless willingness to embrace emerging technologies that have the potential to swiftly enhance their quality of life.

The paradigm shift towards accelerated product adoption

Based on an article cited in visualcapitalist.com regarding the increasing pace of technological adoption since the 1990s, a consistent pattern becomes evident. The entirety of rapidly-adopted technologies are interconnected with the internet. This criterion has been instrumental in driving exponential growth over the past four decades.

The internet and its associated products exhibit a notably accelerated pace of adoption. As an illustration, the increased prevalence of smartphones and tablets has resulted in a considerable surge in social media usage. Nevertheless, the rate of adoption and reach of various internet-related technologies may vary. An illustration of this can be seen in the case of podcasting and e-book readers, both of which have reached a saturation point upon reaching approximately 30% market penetration.

This leads us to the second criterion for achieving rapid expansion, which entails that the necessity be valid in order to ensure widespread adoption. While it is true that not every individual possesses an inclination towards engaging with podcasts or utilizing e-book readers, it cannot be denied that in this day and age, the reliance on mobile devices for internet connectivity is universally imperative.

Finally, regardless of the product's convenience through online accessibility and the existence of a genuine demand, it remains imperative for it to be financially within reach for the broader consumer base. Take into consideration examples such as Spotify, Netflix, Uber/Grab, and the like. These products satisfy the three specifications.

Attainable and commercially viable through online connectivity

A genuine necessity that addresses a tangible issue.

Affordability (subscription-based model)

"In the preceding chapter, I had elucidated three prognostications that may prospects that may arise from a post-Covid-19 epoch:

The prevalence of remote work (and its impact on daily living) is increasingly apparent. For prospective investors, this implies that exploring remote working solutions such as Zoom, as well as remote entertainment options like

Spotify, Netflix, and DIS, etc., could potentially yield profitable results.

The growth of e-commerce sales will come about at an accelerated pace. Examine robust e-commerce platforms such as Amazon and Alibaba. Facebook, too, is introducing the Facebook Shop feature in order to secure a share of the market.

The momentum of digital payment trends is poised to increase rapidly. Examine credit cards such as Visa and Mastercard, along with online payment gateways like PayPal, Stripe, and Square. In Australia, there appears to be a noticeable increase in the number of enterprises providing services that enable individuals to divide their online purchases into several payments for a specified charge. Examples of such offerings include Afterpay and Zip Co, the latter of which recently obtained US-based QuadPay, among others.

11. Reducing Workload and Overseeing Large-scale Operations

In situations where there is a scarcity of water, individuals often exhibit behaviors such as conserving it, stockpiling it, or regarding it as a highly valuable resource, surpassing even the value attributed to gold. Nearly every member of the family is experiencing great unease, fearing that the local water authority may cease its supply in an attempt to regulate it, within a matter of hours or even minutes. The pleasantries of the morning are overlooked, replaced by the clamor of admonishments directed at the children or younger members of the household.

In situations of water abundance, individuals exhibit minimal concern for it. They negligently permit the unattended flow of water and tolerate a prolonged period of leakage without promptly engaging a plumber for its repair.

Financial resources adhere to the same protocol. When faced with scarcity or reduced income, individuals become highly anxious and exhibit a frenetic behavior akin to untamed creatures. When it becomes accessible, the proprietors exhibit profligate behavior and squander it without any discernment. This notion holds validity for individuals, corporations, as well as governmental entities.

Insufficient financial resources, akin to a scarcity of water, present a significant predicament, while an excessive abundance of money gives rise to even more daunting challenges. Similar to the flow of water, money begins to dissipate through various channels and the possessor gradually succumbs to a lack of proportion, rationality, and logic in its management. Managing a limited amount of money (or water) can be effortlessly accomplished, whereas handling an excessive amount of money (or water) poses a significant challenge.

12.

Contrarian Investing

Contrarian investing entails adopting an opposing stance to prevailing market sentiments and trends. Contrarian investors strategically purchase stocks during periods of widespread panic and sell-offs, as they possess the knowledge that a significant influx of stock sales indicates the market is either reaching or has reached its lowest point and will subsequently commence its recovery. They offer their shares for sale in the event of investors exhibiting excessive levels of optimism, as heightened buyer activity generally indicates that the market is at or approaching a pinnacle, signaling an imminent decline.

Contrarians frequently seek out surveys and polls that demonstrate a pronounced inclination towards either excessive optimism or excessive pessimism among the general investor population. Contrarians, adhering to the principle that widespread consensus is indicative of error, will undertake actions diametrically opposed to the recommendations put forth by surveys. They will, in essence, purchase shares when the prevailing sentiment is to sell, and sell when the prevailing sentiment is to buy. It is a pervasive belief to engage in the practice of purchasing assets when their value is depressed and disposing of them when their value is inflated, commonly referred to as the maxim "Buy Low, and Sell High," or the adage that opportune moments for investment arise amidst market turmoil.

We unanimously assent to this without raising any objections, however, the number of investors who genuinely adhere to this principle remains uncertain.

In the month of January 2008, when the Nifty index reached a value of 6350, could you please share the number of investors within your knowledge who opted to sell their holdings at that particular level? When Nifty reached a low of 2250 in the month of October in that particular year, how many investors do you know of who promptly contacted their brokers to make multiple purchases? Only a small number of individuals known to us are likely to have taken action. All others, paralyzed by avarice, likely awaited the Nifty's rise to 8000 or anticipated its subsequent decline to 1800 with trepidation, as denoted by their apprehensive silence. Even the most reputable analysts, who appeared on multiple television channels, unanimously projected the Nifty's next level to be at 1800.

These are cycles. In these cycles, wealth is transferred from less affluent individuals to individuals of greater financial capacity. Even though individuals may have purchased at the 2250 level, it is highly likely that they did not exercise patience with regards to the Nifty index, neither when it reached 6000 nor 8000. This is because when the index increased from 2250 to 3000 and subsequently dropped back to 2500, a significant number of investors who had initially purchased at 2250 chose to sell at 2500, driven by concerns that it may once again decline to levels at or below 2250.

Expressed eloquently, one might state: "Verbalizing contrary viewpoints may be effortless, but embodying the role of a contrarian proves to be an arduous endeavor." What precisely entails a contrarian approach? According to the information provided on Wikipedia, a contrarian is an individual who seeks to generate profit by deviating from conventional wisdom when the consensus opinion is deemed to be incorrect. A contrarian holds the belief that specific patterns of collective conduct exhibited by investors can result in opportunities to exploit misvaluation in the financial markets."

It is human nature. Hardly few walk alone. They desire to align themselves with the collective. In order to go against prevailing beliefs, it is imperative to possess a resolute determination. It may not appeal to every individual's personal preferences. However, numerous individuals actively seek an absolute valuation for stocks rather than solely focusing on relative valuation. Contrarians frequently exhibit a predisposition for value-oriented investing. Mr. Warren Buffet can be regarded as one of the most accomplished contrarian investors.

He invests in stocks that have consistently outperformed over the years. In recent times, he made the acquisition of dwindling stocks of energy corporations that have been witnessing a decline since 2011. The outcome of his investment can only be determined with time, but it is certain that Mr. Buffet meticulously adhered to all crucial market principles before making the decision to purchase energy stocks.

Upon reflection of the paragraph I previously wrote, and during my current editing of the final proof, it has come to my attention that Mr. Buffet's decision to invest in energy stocks has proven to be astute. Over the past year, such stocks have demonstrated superior performance when compared to other sectors. The price of crude oil, which previously fluctuated between $30 and

$40, has now surpassed $70, resulting in positive performance for energy stocks.

Typically, it is the contrarians who truly reap financial gains in the market. They possess exceptional instinct, possess a preference for solitude, and demonstrate the courage to take action at opportune moments while others remain hesitant. They possess not only the exceptional intuition for understanding crowd psychology in extreme situations but also the courage to take action while others hesitate.

Individuals do not bestow you with esteem when you adopt a contrarian stance. It is perceived by others that you have exhibited behavior deemed irrational, leading them to ridicule you for diverging from the majority.

Deviating from the prevailing trend could have adverse consequences, as it may result in a miscalculation of the opportune moments to adopt a contrary stance. An authentic contrarian maintains faith in oneself and remains unperturbed by the opinions or actions of others. On occasion, when one makes an early decision, it may entail a longer waiting period before reaping the rewards. Nevertheless, the annals of history bear witness to the fact that contrarians have consistently achieved substantial profits. Contrarians are always willing to exercise patience in order to substantiate their correctness.

What is Your Why?

Like any pursuit in life, you will always achieve the most success when you establish the underlying purpose or motivation behind your actions. May I inquire as to the rationale behind your actions? Furthermore I don't

Signifying utmost significance, it implies elemental assurance, financial stability, or even liberation from the relentless pursuit of success, albeit in a truly remarkable manner. What is the rationale behind your desire for financial security or liberation from the daily grind? Delve deep! As you contemplate, I shall present a few scenarios to illustrate the implications of delving further into your underlying reasons.

Suppose you are required to transform into a flipper. What is the primary motivation behind the desire of the majority to engage in property flipping? Response: to accumulate substantial financial gains. OK, that is legitimate. However, what is your underlying motivation for seeking considerable financial gain? The significance of this matter stems from the fact that flipping can pose significant difficulties. Should you encounter substantial challenges or setbacks while engaging in the practice of property flipping, it is imperative that you possess a highly compelling rationale for requiring a considerable amount of funds to significantly impact your situation. If your rationale is not robust, there is a substantial likelihood that you may not endure the adversities.

Consider this scenario: You were brought up in a state of genuine poverty. Your family had limited means to support you, which consequently hindered your educational progress and impeded the formation of healthy interpersonal connections in certain instances. Currently, you are an adult who has progeny of your own.

Due to your personal experiences and understanding the hardships of growing up in poverty without adequate support, you are determined to shield your children from such experiences. You come to understand that engaging in property flipping can provide your family with a level of accommodation previously unattainable. This is your underlying motivation: striving tirelessly to shield your children from experiencing the same hardships you endured.

If you subsequently engage in property flipping endeavors and encounter potentially favorable outcomes initially, only to face a significant obstacle soon after, how determined would you be to devise solutions and surmount said hurdle? If the sustenance of your entire family hinges upon the outcome of your endeavors, it can be surmised that you will be highly compelled to attain success. The underlying motivation in this context is profound, as your ability to succeed not only determines the financial well-being of both you and your children, a matter of significant magnitude in its own right, but it also serves as a catalyst for personal catharsis, addressing the scars of your own childhood experiences.

I will provide you with my personal rationale for this. Throughout, my underlying motivation has consistently revolved around the pursuit of opportunities. It could be argued that I have a strong preoccupation with the concept of opportunity. I must determine my preferences, timing, and approach to execute tasks as desired. I frequently share the narrative of being the sole individual in Los Angeles who operates a manual transmission vehicle, despite the notoriously slow and congested nature of the city's traffic conditions. I operate a manual transmission vehicle because

I do not require my transmission to provide me with instructions; rather, I require the ability to initiate movement at will. I acknowledge that pursuing this opportunity might be deemed driven by emotion, nevertheless, I want to convey that one could argue I am extremely passionate about it. I, too, become fatigued while driving, therefore relocating provides me with an activity. An alternative model is when I first joined my school's rugby team as a novice. In accordance with the established norms of many sports teams, freshmen are typically subjected to disciplinary actions by the seasoned players throughout their initial year. It dates back as far as a fraternity. The outcome of assisting veterans in obtaining what they required, as directed by me, was not realized.

Eventually, the seasoned individuals determined that it was fruitless to offer me any form of guidance or counsel. Even in the present day, there remains a significant probability that upon receiving an instruction from you, I shall either fail to comply or exhibit a complete deviation from the prescribed action. I, in no way, exhibit rudeness in this matter. I am fully conscious and understanding of the situation, and if you happen to hold a position of true authority over me, I will undoubtedly show utmost respect towards it. However, aside from that, I establish my own principles, an expression of personal liberties in my perspective.

For me, freedom stands as an unshakable rationale of paramount significance. The extent of my contentment is directly correlated to the degree of freedom I am afforded. If there happens to be any aspect of my life where I fall beneath the expectations set by another individual, and it is preferable for me not to remain in such a position, I will prepare myself accordingly and make diligent efforts to seize opportunities for improvement in that particular area. If I hadn't possessed such an exceptional pursuit for opportunity, I would not have persisted in business for the duration that I have. Business can be incredibly challenging and exhilarating, like navigating through a relentless and dynamic environment. However, even amidst the most challenging circumstances, I recognized that I had an imperative to strategize and overcome the impediment, as failure to do so would compromise my autonomy. In the event that I were ever to consider reverting back to conventional employment, I would be required to conform to the authority, priorities, objectives, and schedules set by another individual. No singular entity signifies opportunity to me. In the challenging moments of contemplation regarding my ability to advance as an entrepreneurial visionary, I inexorably sense an obligation to persist. As a result of its inherent robustness, it leaves me with no alternative but to endure. This is the method through which the solidity of your rationale ought to be experienced.

Authentic testamentary planning does not solely revolve around monetary assets. It pertains to what can be acquired with the cash. I have never encountered an individual who genuinely desired money without a valid underlying reason for requiring those funds. What is your plan for handling the cash once it is obtained?

Support your family or a person in your immediate circle.

Grant yourself the opportunity to pursue early retirement, thereby granting you the ability to

Please provide the necessary information.

Demonstrate your worth to someone, even though ultimately it is a personal endeavor wherein your own beliefs and convictions play a critical role, with potential individuals including your parents or those who may have doubted your capabilities.

Allocate time towards participating in philanthropic activities and actively contributing to the betterment of society.

Supporting causes that ignite your passion

Within one of those possibilities lies the answer to your question. I am inclined towards opting for early retirement, as retirement traditionally signifies freedom and aligns with the lifestyle I aspire to - one without fixed schedules, where I have autonomy to pursue my own desires and am not accountable to anyone.

If you have yet to ascertain the exact purpose behind your actions, engaging in a constructive academic exercise would be to deliberate upon the underlying rationale. Refrain from dwelling on the question of why, and instead direct your thoughts towards contemplating your ultimate aspirations. What are the primary elements that hold significant importance in your life, both inherently and for the overall trajectory of your life? Should you require anything, may I inquire as to what that might entail, in general? If you were creating a vision board encompassing your life aspirations, what elements would it comprise? When conceiving the multitude of necessities, direct your focus towards seeking a subject matter. What commonalities do those things possess for all practical purposes? Do they specifically cater to opportunities, like they do in my current circumstances, or do they primarily focus on aspects such as security and stability? Or then again euphoria. Or then again status. Encapsulated within those desires lies the core reason for your actions. You may not readily ascertain the reason for your actions at once—occasionally, it may take years to truly comprehend the purpose behind them. However, by maintaining vigilance towards it, you will acquire a deeper comprehension of the purpose behind your actions, thereby facilitating your path towards achieving greater success.

An Invitation

I have recently launched Vodyssey, an online platform at www.Vodyssey.com, which serves as a coaching and mentoring platform focused on equipping individuals with a systematic blueprint to construct their own lucrative Lifestyle Asset portfolio. We provide support to individuals in bridging the gap between

I am considering making a reservation for a vacation rental and am inclined to proceed with submitting the payment.

We present a meticulously devised strategy, accessible to anyone, for creating, maintaining, and promoting a profitable portfolio of vacation rentals.

This is an exhilarating period for both my family and me as we embark on the endeavor of incorporating Lifestyle Assets into our portfolio. Moreover, we have the unique opportunity to contribute significantly to raising awareness and enabling others to reap the benefits of incorporating Lifestyle Assets into their own lives.

Both Wyatt and Grace diligently engage in the practice of daily diary writing. At the culmination of one of Wyatt's journal entries elucidating his daily activities, he expressed, "I am leading an existence that embodies the utmost magnificence bestowed upon a juvenile."

I could not have been more elated by his sentiment.

I extend an invitation for your esteemed presence to accompany us on this sojourn, and I extend a warm invitation for you to commence living the most superlative existence attainable.

Day Trading Options With Momentum"

This particular approach to options day trading entails placing trades based on the price volatility and the rate at which volume changes. The term's usage stems from the fact that the underlying concept of the strategy revolves around the notion that the momentum driving the price action of the correlated asset is sufficient to maintain its movement in the same trajectory. This phenomenon occurs due to the tendency for investors to be drawn to assets that experience price appreciation, leading to further increases in their value. Individuals engaged in options day trading, employing this strategy, capitalize on the prevailing momentum to generate a profit based on anticipated price fluctuations.

This approach is predicated on the utilization of technical analysis to monitor the fluctuations in the pricing of the correlated asset. This analysis provides the day trader with a comprehensive overview that encompasses momentum indicators such as:

The Momentum Indicator calculates the strength of the price movement as a trend by utilizing the most recently recorded closing price of the corresponding asset.

The Relative Strength Index (RSI) represents a measure of gains and losses observed during a specified timeframe.

Moving Averages enable the day trader to examine previous fluctuations and assess the patterns observed in the market.

The Stochastic Oscillator is a method of evaluating the recent closing prices of a given asset within a predetermined timeframe.

The efficacy and simplicity of momentum-based options day trading are contingent upon its proper execution. The day trader must remain updated on current news and earnings reports in order to make well-informed decisions utilizing this particular trading strategy.

Day Trading Strategies for Reversing Positions

This approach is predicated on contrarian trading and fundamentally contradicts the principles of momentum-based options day trading. Commonly referred to as trend trading or pull back trending, this strategy is executed by options day traders who possess the ability to discern retracements occurring in opposition to the prevailing price trends. Undoubtedly, this course of action carries inherent risks, yet it holds the potential for substantial profitability in the event of a favorable outcome. Due to the requisite level of market knowledge and trading experience necessary to execute this strategy proficiently, it is advised against for neophytes to undertake.

This strategy adopts a bullish stance towards options trading, involving the purchase of an out of the money call option alongside the sale of an out of the money put option. The potential for unlimited gains and losses exists in equal measure.

Employing Options Day Trading Strategies with a Scalping Approach

This particular trading methodology pertaining to options encompasses the act of purchasing and subsequently selling the identical affiliated asset on multiple occasions within a single trading day. This proves advantageous in the presence of pronounced market volatility. The profitability of an options day trader lies in purchasing an options position at a lower cost, subsequently selling it at a higher value, or alternatively, selling the options position at a higher value and then purchasing it at a lower value, thus contingent upon the nature of the option (call or put).

This particular method of options trading is heavily dependent on the availability of liquidity. Illiquid options are not suitable for implementation within this trading style, as the options day trader must have the capacity to initiate and terminate such trades multiple times within a single day.

Engaging in the trading of liquid options enables day traders to achieve optimal profitability both upon entering and exiting trades.

The conventional approach involves engaging in multiple small-scale options trades throughout the day as a means to garner profits, as opposed to infrequently executing larger trades. Engaging in substantial trading using this specific approach has the potential to result in significant financial losses within a short span of a few hours. Hence, this approach is exclusively advised for diligent options day traders who are satisfied with pursuing modest, repetitive gains, despite its comparatively lower risk profile in contrast to alternative strategies.

Owing to the inherent characteristics of this methodology, it represents the most concise variant of options day trading, as it encompasses a duration of merely a few hours, rather than the entirety of the day. Individuals who engage in this method of day trading are commonly referred to as scalpers. The evaluation of the optimal investment opportunities in relation to the price fluctuations of the relevant assets necessitates the utilization of technical analysis.

Scalping is a general term that encompasses various techniques employed for the purpose of scalp trading. There are instances of time and sales scalping in which day traders utilize historical data of executed, disposed, and annulled transactions to ascertain the most favorable trading opportunities and ideal timing for these transactions. Alternative variants of scalping entail the utilization of bars and charts to conduct an examination of future trends.

Your inaugural foray into real estate investment

Engaging in your initial real estate transaction, whether for personal accommodation or for investment purposes, can be both fulfilling and exhilarating, yet it can also evoke feelings of apprehension. Upon embarking on your journey in real estate investment, adhere to the following series of actions.

1. Inform yourself. This does not entail a mandate for you to re-enroll in educational institutions, however, you must acknowledge accountability for your actions.

Require comprehensive understanding and diligent examination of the subject. Conduct a thorough market analysis for the desired industry you aspire to penetrate. Retrieve comparable property sales prices through online resources.

official land records maintained at the local level, as well as the services provided by local professional real estate agents. Gain knowledge about the transaction process, the roles and duties of each individual involved, legal mandates, as well as insurance protocols.

Each constituent exhibits diverse rates, and through diligent examination of pricing, one can preempt financial losses.

2. Arrange your finance. One common mistake often committed by individuals who are new to a particular task is

Investors should first search for a property and then proceed to secure financing. Prior to embarking on your quest for the elusive treasure, it is advisable to secure pre-approval for financing. "Select a lending institution by opting for a bank,

Mortgage institution, or online lending service.

When you have a meeting with your lender, communicate the exact amount of investment you intend to make. They will gather comprehensive financial data pertaining to your personal circumstances, including details about your income, credit history, and liabilities. Subsequently, they will apprise you of the findings, providing you with a thorough assessment.

much they\\\'ll finance.

Given the wide range of financing alternatives presently accessible, it is imperative to ascertain which one is most suitable for your circumstances.

The financing plans encompass various components, including interest rates, initial cash

investment, and tax consequences.

3. Locate your property. It could prove challenging to ascertain

profitable real estate. Utilize the internet and the "Real Estate" category.

segment of the local publication. Seek out properties that have been foreclosed upon or are available for rental. Conduct a thorough exploration of the designated vicinity to identify residential properties that are being sold directly by the owners.

4. Make efforts to attain an equitable resolution. Once you have identified the perfect residence, it will be necessary to engage in negotiations in order to secure the most favorable price.

Do not anticipate the reception of a favorable bargain. Sellers seek to optimize the monetary value of their property, while buyers aspire to minimize the financial expenditure involved in the transaction. Successful negotiation requires engaging in a collaborative process with the seller to achieve a mutually beneficial resolution. Exhibit assertiveness coupled with a willingness to compromise. The lack of adaptability often gives rise to both financial setbacks and heightened levels of anxiety.

Fundamentals of the 529 Plan

The 529 college plan is a crucial government initiative utilized by a multitude of families. I highly recommend this program if you are beginning to explore options for establishing a college fund for your child. Having been commenced in 1996, this tax program was initially scheduled for expiration a few years ago. However, owing to its exceptional success and its swift adoption as an essential requirement among numerous American households, it is highly probable that this program will persist indefinitely.

The 529 college plan serves as a means to allocate funds for your child's education. Nevertheless, alongside this savings plan, there are certain pivotal regulations to be aware of. This funding is exclusively designated for the purpose of higher education, and consequently, if accessed prematurely, it is subject to taxation as ordinary income. If you happen to be devoid of college expenses, whether by means of scholarships or other forms of financial assistance, the sole manner in which funds can be withdrawn from the account would be to incur associated fees. Aside from any taxes remitted to state or federal authorities, an supplementary levy of ten percent is imposed for non-utilization of the funds towards the purpose of education. These penalties carry significant weight when it comes to withdrawing funds for purposes unrelated to education, therefore it is advisable to exercise prudence while setting aside funds. I would recommend setting aside funds to cover approximately a quarter of the total tuition expenses for your child's four-year college education.

The advantages of the 529 plan lie in the fact that any withdrawals from the account remain exempt from taxation by both the federal and state governments. However, it is advisable to consult IRS Publication 970 to ensure that this statement holds true for your unique situation. Funds held within a 529 account are also portable between different states. No matter if you commence the plan in New York and subsequently relocate to California, or regardless of the eventual path life may traverse, the plan's advantages will be universally attainable. It is worth mentioning that the plan does possess additional value in states where an income tax is levied. You will continue to enjoy the advantages of exempting federal income tax on funds that are withdrawn from a 529 account for educational purposes. However, the additional benefit of evading state income tax is a crucial aspect that contributes significantly to the allure of this particular tax shelter.

One notable benefit of the 529 plan, particularly for novice investors, lies in its effortless ability to serve as an auxiliary component to your broader financial investments. A 529 plan will accrue returns akin to those of a mutual fund. Your particular state will carefully choose a limited number of investment options with the aim of achieving returns that surpass the prevailing interest rate. It is highly probable that the fund will indeed achieve this, and the likelihood of success in this regard rises as the duration of the funds' storage in the account extends. Funds can also be transferred directly from the bank account to your savings account, thereby reducing concerns regarding the initial amount required for commencing savings for your child's education.

Optimal Utilization of 529 Plan

The imposition of both a ten percent penalty and income tax by federal and state authorities renders the 529 plan a prudent option for opting to invest an amount that is lower than your anticipated requirements. It is imperative to exercise caution in this matter, as it is widely acknowledged that college education entails exorbitant costs. Nevertheless, it is necessary to formulate certain conjectures regarding the extent of financial support your child will be able to provide. It is recommended as a conventional practice to endeavor saving for approximately 25% of your child's educational expenses. Based on the projected figures of $378,000 for private universities and $168,000 for public universities by 2034, the potential savings range from $42,000 to $94,500. These figures should appear considerably less alarming than the total cost over a four-year period, albeit still significant financial obligations. One should approach the utilization of a savings plan such as the 529 by carefully analyzing each deposit and its contribution towards achieving the ultimate objective.

To ensure adequate funds for a private four-year tuition in 2034, it would be prudent to allocate a monthly contribution of $204, which will accumulate to approximately one quarter of the anticipated cost. The monthly deposit requirement for public schools amounts to a mere $91. These figures should be considerably more comprehensible, and it is hoped that you are now recognizing the merits of the 529 plan. It is understandable to have concerns about the disparity in financial resources between the savings account and the educational needs of your child.

We are only accumulating sufficient funds to remain $126,000 below the total expense of a public school, and $283,000 below the expenditure associated with a private school. Do not allow the magnitude of these numbers to dishearten you; there are numerous means by which this gap can be bridged.

Engaging in a quick search for scholarships can result in securing significant financial assistance for your child. Based on your economic circumstances (with the primary consideration being whether or not you are a homeowner), it is possible for your child to be eligible for financial assistance, which does not necessitate repayment. Furthermore, this issue is adversely affecting numerous households simultaneously, leading to an escalated endeavor in mitigating these financial burdens. Although the decrease in college education costs is unlikely to occur in the near future, the emergence of more astute alternatives is progressively gaining traction.

An emerging concept that has gained significant traction in recent years involves enrolling one's child within a local community college to complete the initial two years of their academic pursuit. Community colleges are substantially more cost-effective in comparison to both private and public institutions, providing the fundamental courses required for the initial two years of a college education. Furthermore, community schools also offer the advantage of extended residence with family for an additional two years. Although this may not be preferable for you or your child, it does provide significant cost savings of approximately $10,000-14,000 per year on living expenditures. Finally, I would like to highlight an essential aspect that often goes unnoticed - in addition to providing quality education, community colleges often exhibit a phenomenon of grade inflation. Should your child choose to pursue enrollment in a well-regarded four-year university subsequent to completing community college, it is highly probable that they shall be able to effectuate a transfer, leveraging their commendable academic achievements over a period of two years. This commendable grade point average may enhance their eligibility for additional scholarship opportunities during their remaining two years and enhance their appeal as a transfer candidate to an institution of even greater prestige.

The foundation of the 529 plan lies solely in long-term investment strategies, thus necessitating rules that align with terms ranging from eighteen to twenty years. The implementation of the plan will be portable across state borders, thereby presenting no hindrance to initiating a 529 plan for your child, regardless of your residential relocation. The sole challenges associated with this savings plan arise in the event that the funds are not utilized for educational purposes. Before proceeding, it is essential to precisely define this aspect. The educational expenses funded through a 529 plan are not limited exclusively to those incurred for the benefit of your own child. It is equally applicable to both oneself or a cherished individual, and does not necessitate association with a conventional higher education qualification. It possesses utility in both vocational education institutions or postgraduate academic institutions. These are all factors to consider and bear in mind when determining the optimal utilization of the 529 plan to suit your individual circumstances.

3. OWNING OVERVALUED STOCKS

The primary objective of value investing is to acquire assets at a low cost and subsequently sell them at a higher price, or alternatively, retain them until their intrinsic value is realized. Pursuing a flawed approach of miscalculating and investing in already overpriced stocks undermines the fundamental objective.

It is not advisable to pay beyond or precisely the appropriate value for stocks, as this does not align with the principles of gaining profits. To maximize profitability, it is recommended to strive for lower purchase prices. The complete realization of value investing cannot be achieved by confining your investments to the safety zone, as elucidated in the preceding chapters.

One intriguing aspect of the stock market is the recurring phenomenon where one individual's purchase prompts another's sale, with each party harboring the belief of their own shrewdness.

William Feather

4. INABILITY TO DIVERSIFY

It is widely understood that consolidating all resources in a single effort entails significant risk. It is also applicable to the principles of value investing. To mitigate the potential for financial loss, it is advisable to distribute your investments across a diverse range of industries and companies. By taking such action, in the event that a specific company or industry experiences a significant blow, you can rely on your alternative investments for support.

A diversified portfolio does not necessarily require 100 stocks; rather, investing in a range of 10 stocks across different industries can also achieve diversification. Additionally, it is prudent to carefully select a small number of exceptional stocks and allocate a significant portion of capital to them over a designated timeframe in order to maximize investment returns.

5. FLOWING IN EMOTIONS

Frequently, it is observed that temptation eclipses feeble intellects and compels them to engage in unseemly actions. For example, in the event that you make a purchase of stocks and subsequently observe a decline in their value, it may be instinctive to succumb to fear and promptly sell them in order to minimize potential losses. However, it is imperative to maintain composure and approach the situation with a level-headed and logical mindset, considering the broader, long-term perspective.

Take into consideration whether this is a temporary or enduring circumstance. Is the company or industry equipped to address this issue within a 12-month timeframe? What does the future hold for this company? Is there a possibility that the loss cannot be regained? Please respond to these inquiries prior to initiating any action.

Procedures for Acquiring NFTs

In essence, it is possible to procure any digital image as a non-fungible token (NFT). However, there are several factors to take into consideration when purchasing one, particularly if you are a novice. You must make a determination regarding which marketplace to purchase from, the specific digital wallet necessary for storage, and the particular type of cryptocurrency required in order to finalize the transaction.

Several prevalent NFT marketplaces encompass OpenSea, Mintable, Nifty Gateway, and Rarible. Additionally, there exist specialized marketplaces catering to specific types of NFTs. Examples include NBA Top Shot, which focuses on basketball video highlights, and Valuables, which facilitates auctions for tweets, such as Dorsey's presently being offered for bidding. However, exercise caution regarding charges. Certain marketplaces impose a 'gas' fee, representing the energy consumption necessary for the execution of the transaction on the blockchain. Additional charges may encompass the expenses associated with currency conversion from dollars to ethereum (the prevailing cryptocurrency used for purchasing NFTs) and concluding fees.

If you are curious and desire to acquire additional insight into the process of purchasing an NFT, we have undertaken the initiative and procured one ourselves. (And indeed, it is a feline companion.)

Priced into the market

Assuming a company is executing a major product launch, there is a prevailing notion that the launch will successfully transpire...

... One might opine that it would be advantageous to consider investing in stocks at this juncture, wouldn't they?

The issue at hand is that the positive information regarding the product launch is expected to be incorporated into the existing market prices. This implies that once a limited number of individuals become aware of the potential success of the product launch, the stock price experiences an increase. For those who are new to this, it is typically too late to derive any advantage from making a purchase at this point.

EBITDA

EBITDA is an acronym denoting 'Earnings Before Interest, Taxes, Depreciation, and Amortization'. It reflects the extent of the company's gross income.

By the way, it should be noted that 'Amortisation' is a term with dual interpretations. When an asset is amortized, it involves allocating a monetary value to it for the purpose of financial record-keeping. If one opts to amortize a debt, it entails gradually repaying it over a specified duration.

MT4/MT5

Represents the abbreviation for the platforms known as 'MetaTrader 4/MetaTrader 5'. These platforms are freely available for professional usage and are occasionally granted access by certain brokers. Not for newbies!

P/E ratio

'Price-to-Earnings' ratio. This method of company valuation is widely recognized and employed. The phrase denotes the quotient obtained by dividing the price of a single share in a corporation by the corporation's earnings per share (EPS). Companies exhibiting elevated P/E ratios are regarded as costly. Companies with comparatively low price-to-earnings ratios can be considered to have attractive valuations.

Spreads

The term 'spread' denotes the disparity between the purchase price of an asset through a broker and its selling price. Frequently denoted as a 'bid/ask spread,' it is advantageous to seek a minimal spread. Alternatively, if the price fluctuates, a portion or potentially all of your potential profit will be eroded due to the spread.

Exemplary illustration of a spread: the current valuation of stock A stands at $100. A broker could potentially present a range of $95-$105 as a spread. This implies that Stock A can be purchased at a price of $105 (resulting in a $5 commission paid to the broker), or can be sold at a price of $95 (resulting in a $5 commission paid to the broker). Brokers generate profit through the utilization of spreads.

Stop Loss

Cease losses have the potential to prevent catastrophic outcomes. When utilizing a "cease loss" strategy, your online brokerage's software will execute an automatic sale of the asset if its price declines beyond a designated threshold. This safeguard prevents excessive financial loss in the event of a sudden and significant decline in the value of an asset.

The Principle of the One Percent: "The Guideline of the One Percent: "The One Percent Doctrine: "The One Percent Standard: "The Rule of the One Percent:

When it comes to assessing a rental property, this is a customary practice that individuals typically adhere to. Let it be posited that the gross monthly rent (revenue prior to deductions) shall amount to no less than 1% of the purchase price. Subsequently, I would recommend conducting a more comprehensive assessment of the investment. Nevertheless, in the event that it does not, it would be advisable to disregard it.

As an example,

If the price of the house you are considering amounts to $200,000 and we employ this approach, the monthly rent would be required to reach $2,000. If the rental fee falls below one percent, it fails to meet the criteria of one percent.

Based on this regulation, the residential property is expected to yield an annual gross income equivalent to approximately 12% of the total acquisition cost.

Nevertheless, once all expenses are deducted, the property is projected to yield a net income equivalent to approximately 6 to 8% of the initial purchase price.

Typically, this represents a satisfactory yield; however, it is contingent upon the specific locality in question. The rental yield tends to be lower in the more affluent areas, whereas it typically increases in neighborhoods considered less desirable.

In the absence of compounding interest, any percentage gain you earn will be devoid of significance. In order to enhance the potential growth of your profits through investments in the stock market, it is advisable to reinvest a substantial portion, around one hundred percent, of your revenues. This will enable your gains to experience compounding effects and facilitate an increase in overall profitability.

ROI

Return on Investment (ROI) encompasses the rental income derived from your investments, in addition to the appreciation in the value of the property, encompassing residential dwellings, commercial structures, and undeveloped land.

Suppose that you are planning to invest an amount of $20,000 into a property that has an ultimate valuation of $140,000. In that case, the investment value shall correspond to the initial amount you have contributed. Nevertheless, it is imperative to avoid the mistake of including the entire real estate investment, as it will enable you to capitalize on your finances. By making a lesser initial investment in the form of a down payment for your investment, you will wield a greater degree of influence over the value, as the entirety of the return on investment from the property will be acquired by you. It will come to your attention that the aforementioned property will yield a commensurate return on investment of approximately 15%. A mere 15% of a sum totaling $20,000 corresponds to a modest amount of $3,000.

The return on investment (ROI) shall be determined by means of dividing the amount acquired by the amount invested, and subsequently multiplying the outcome by one hundred.

Return on investment based on appreciation in capital: The appreciation in the value of the property will contribute to the capital gain. Whether or not you decide to sell the property, it will still be possible for you to ascertain its present value.

Should you decide to, you have the option of enlisting the services of a certified appraiser. Nevertheless, capital gains tax shall be imposed on any undeveloped land or buildings that are intended to be leased to tenants.

In order to determine the return on investment, it is necessary to divide the initial investment amount by the appreciation in property value, and subsequently multiply the quotient by a factor of one hundred.

Trading ETFs

Financiers who regularly purchase or sell shares in an ETF are required to pay a commission to the financial institution for each transaction. When purchasing or selling ETF shares, the investor is able to obtain the prevailing market price at the moment the order is executed. The price may fluctuate throughout the trading day. On the other hand, a collective investment vehicle determines its net asset value on a daily basis. When purchasing or redeeming shares of a mutual fund, the price you receive is based on the net asset value calculated after your order has been placed. The intraday evaluation of ETFs generally offers investors increased trading flexibility given that they can monitor price performance in real-time, eliminating the need to wait until the end of the day to determine their purchase or sale price.

Similarly, by employing diverse investment strategies, it is feasible to generate profits through ETFs provided that you sell your shares at a value higher than the purchase price. You also stand to reap advantages if the safeguards within an ETF generate interest or profits. The payment can be either reinvested or distributed to investors on a quarterly or annual basis, depending on the structure of the ETF. Similarly, there is a possibility for an ETF's value to decline. Naturally, in the event that the value decreases and you decide to divest, you could incur a financial loss.

In sharp contrast to jointly owned assets, the acquisition of ETFs using leverage presents a viable opportunity to execute trades at prices lower than their actual worth. These advanced speculative procedures may prove valuable to certain experienced investors; nonetheless, for other investors, the costs and risks associated with such tactics may outweigh the potential benefits.

When investing in ETFs, it is customary to incur transaction costs for each trade, much like what is observed with individual stocks. Therefore, it is generally not recommended to utilize ETFs in strategies such as dollar-cost averaging for long-term investing purposes. The transaction costs incurred for each purchase or sale could significantly diminish the overall investment return. The same cautionary advice pertains to collectively owned assets that impose front-end sales charges.

A number of ETF providers have initiated the provision of no-commission ETFs. While this may prove advantageous for investors aiming to carry out multiple small transactions, it is important to note that the absence of commission should not be the sole determinant in the decision-making process regarding which ETF to purchase. It is necessary for you to thoroughly examine the fine print regarding no-cost exchanges (wherein a particular firm levies a fee if you purchase a no-commission ETF and proceed to sell it within 30 days of acquisition). Additionally, as we have demonstrated earlier, it is important to take into account the expense ratios associated with ETFs, which represent a separate form of cost that can accumulate.

ETF Expenses

Irrespective of any business commission you may incur, exchange-traded funds (ETFs) possess expense ratios, akin to mutual funds, calculated as a percentage of the assets you have invested. Exchange-traded funds (ETFs) do not incur any loads or 12b-1 expenses (fees deducted annually from the pooled resources of an investment vehicle to cover the costs associated with promoting and distributing the fund to investors).

Typically, actively managed ETFs tend to have higher costs compared to passively managed index ETFs. Before purchasing shares of an ETF, it is advisable to thoroughly review all available information about the ETF, including its prospectus. Upon request, every ETF will provide a comprehensive proposal.

ETFs and Taxes

ETFs can be declared in either accessible, charge-acknowledged, or tax-exempt accounts. According to the information on record, any capital gains derived from the sale of reserve shares are subject to taxation in the year they are obtained. However, it is important to note that the applicable tax rate may be based on your long-term capital gains rate.

Curiously, within a conceded duty account, any expansions are integrated into the total assets of the account and are subjected to regular taxation as income when withdrawn at a later point in time. In a record qualifying for tax-exempt status, any additional contributions or earnings will not incur any obligations provided that the guidelines for withdrawals are followed.

Although generally resulting in lower tax liabilities compared to holding an equivalent mutual fund in the same account, it is important to acknowledge that there may be exceptions with ETFs held within an eligible record. Employed in inverse ETFs may result in potential obligation for charges. Therefore, the aforementioned unusual ETFs, such as certain emerging market funds and precious metals funds classified as "collectibles" by the IRS, are subjected to standard income tax rates for short-term gains and a 28 percent tax rate for long-term gains.

Fundamentals Of Cryptocurrencies

Cryptocurrencies are essentially a form of digital currency designed to fulfill the fundamental purpose of paper currencies: enabling the smooth conduct of transactions and the resolution of financial obligations. Nevertheless, cryptocurrencies are designed to serve a broader purpose than just that. Specifically, the fundamental principle of cryptocurrencies lies in their underlying technological framework commonly referred to as the "blockchain."

The blockchain, referred to as a "digital ledger," is designed with the purpose of promoting accountability and transparency. This implies that users are required to verify transactions in a manner that ensures the presence of a third-party authentication for each transaction. This facilitates a state of transparency where every transaction is documented and incapable of being erased.

The primary purpose of the digital ledger is to establish a trust framework that instills users with the assurance that their interactions are conducted with utmost integrity, thus fostering a sense of confidence. Consequently, the utilization of cryptocurrency is devoid of any undisclosed manipulations or deceptive practices.

The methodology by which the blockchain verifies transactions involves the application of a mathematical algorithm. The equation's solution serves to authenticate the transaction, ensuring its logging and the subsequent release of payment to the recipient of the cryptocurrency.

Initially, this system exhibited exceptional efficiency and demonstrated remarkable ease of administration. This can be attributed to the simplicity of the questions, enabling computers to effortlessly solve them within a mere fraction of a second. Nevertheless, a significant constraint existed whereby every problem could only be employed singularly.

Now, this should not present a concern since there exists an infinitely large pool of mathematical problems that could be employed for authentication purposes. However, challenges would gradually become increasingly complex to resolve. This necessitates not merely an extended duration but also an augmented computational capacity. Thus far, the blockchain, which has functioned as the fundamental technology behind Bitcoin, has effectively reached its conclusion. The blockchain will presently necessitate enormous quantities of computational resources and electrical energy, thereby rendering its long-term viability unattainable.

The advent of alternative cryptocurrencies has sought to address the challenges encountered by Bitcoin. One major concern pertaining to Bitcoin is the generation of new coins through the authentication of transactions. This is called mining. Presently, it is worth noting that not all transactions result in the creation of a fresh unit of currency, especially when preexisting units are employed as a medium of exchange. Nevertheless, the developers of Bitcoin have alluded to implementing a maximum limit on the overall supply of Bitcoin. As of now, there is no definitive figure available, but this factor contributes significantly to the sustained high valuation of Bitcoin.

In order to mitigate potential supply challenges, alternative cryptocurrencies have given rise to a phenomenon commonly referred to as an "initial coin offering" or ICO. An Initial Coin Offering (ICO) can be defined as the introduction of a novel blockchain that generates and releases a series of coins into the market, devoid of the requirement for third-party verification to guarantee its origin. In order to address the concern pertaining to third-party authentication, measures have been implemented wherein the necessity for progressively complex mathematical problems is obviated.

Currently, the number of existing cryptocurrencies surpasses 5,000. Certain currencies fall under the category of niche currencies, primarily employed by gamers within specific gaming platforms. In addition to that particular platform, they serve no purpose. Alternative approaches have been employed by representing them as digital tokens, capable of endorsing specific transactions. An illustrative instance of this phenomenon can be observed in the generation of digital tokens following each instance of conducting an online electronic banking transaction. Your financial institution deploys a verification code to your mobile phone for the purpose of validating and affirming the transaction.

These solutions have been adopted as substitutes for the mechanisms employed in Bitcoin. Ultimately, the resilience of cryptocurrency technology is steadily growing. This holds significant importance for investors, given that the occurrence of the Bitcoin bubble has instilled caution within the cryptocurrency community regarding the potential emergence of another bubble.

Regarding the issues of inflation, interest rates, taxes, and risk

No investor likes inflation. It possesses the capacity to erode your financial gains, regardless of the investment instrument you select. Please be aware that when inflation rises, interest rates tend to increase, which may have implications for your investment interest in stocks.

It is commonly said that death and taxes are inevitable. You can\\\'t avoid either. Nevertheless, it is possible for you to postpone the payment of your taxes. The key to minimizing tax liability as a value investor is to adopt a long-term approach by retaining ownership of stocks, instead of engaging in frequent selling transactions. Due to the phenomenon of compounding, your investment experiences growth. If you exclusively engage in selling for reinvestment purposes, you will incur taxation, thereby impeding the potential benefits of compound interest. With that being stated, however, it is important to avoid retaining the investment excessively and eventually depleting all of your funds. Please ensure that you divest if the company's future outlook appears to be deteriorating.

A decline in both stock prices and interest rates typically occurs in response to perceived decreases in investment returns. When interest rates are reduced, they foster economic expansion and posit the allure of favorable prospects for stock investments. You merely need to acquire knowledge of the stock's intrinsic value through the application of this formula:

The formula for calculating intrinsic value can be represented as: E multiplied by (2g + 8.5) multiplied by 4.4, divided by Y.

Where...

The variable 'E' denotes the yearly income.

r denotes the mean rate of growth.

y represents the rate of interest

When the interest rate surpasses 4.4, the aforementioned expression will yield a value below 1, thereby reducing the intrinsic value. Simultaneously, any interest rate below 4.4 percent signifies positive developments and augments the intrinsic value.

It is important to note that any figure exceeding 5.5 percent is unfavorable, whereas any figure below 5 percent is favorable. Please be aware that the fluctuation of interest rates is inevitable over time, and is contingent upon factors such as inflation, the state of the economy, and the projections of investors.

In regards to the concept of risk, there exist theories that have endeavored to quantify it within investment analysis through the utilization of the Greek letter beta. This beta metric evaluates the valuation of a stock in relation to the general market and the valuation of other stocks. When the beta coefficient is below 1.0, it suggests that there is a possibility of the stock price exhibiting divergent movement or, alternatively, minimal correlation with the broader market movement. It has likely been imparted upon you that investments in low beta stocks carry a higher degree of safety compared to those in high beta stocks.

One notable aspect concerning beta is its insignificance to the value-oriented investor, given that it precisely quantifies the volatility in stock prices, a matter that holds no relevance to your interests. It is imperative for one to solely focus on ascertaining whether the stock price represents an advantageous opportunity or an exceptionally advantageous opportunity in relation to its prospective, enduring worth. Your focal point ought to lie in the overall performance of the company, rather than the comparative performance of its stock in relation to other company stocks.

The sole occasion when beta holds significance is when there is a substantial level of price volatility, as this could indicate a certain degree of uncertainty regarding the company. The associated risks of these stocks frequently become apparent well in advance of examining the beta.

Interest rates, taxes, inflation, and risk have the potential to exert an influence on your investments and decisions. Inflation does not necessarily have to factor into your decision-making process, however, it is prudent to remain vigilant of the potential consequences it may exert on interest rates. Taxes will undeniably have an impact on the management of your investments. The greater the extent to which you postpone them, the higher your long-term return will be, taking into account taxes. Interest rates are influential factors that can contribute to the appreciation or depreciation of your company's valuation as an investment. From the perspective of a value investor, risk pertains more to the future potential of the company rather than its current stock price. In instances where an elevated level of risk is observed, it is natural to have a heightened preference for a greater discount margin of safety between the stock price and the intrinsic value of the stock. It can be challenging to accurately quantify these factors, however, you may consider making modifications in discount rates or seeking higher interest rates prior to allocating your funds.

www.ingramcontent.com/pod-product-compliance
Lightning Source LLC
Chambersburg PA
CBHW071232210326
41597CB00016B/2021